HELLO MOONLIGHT
Love, Sunshine

AMBER L. GRAHAM

Hello Moonlight. Love, Sunshine

Brand It Beautifully™ Book Designs at branditbeautifully.com

ISBN: 978-0-578-94554-5

Printed in the United States of America

TABLE OF CONTENTS

MOONLIGHT

Do you know why I call you my moonlight?

When everything is winding down
And coming to its end, there is you.
I think of you.

When all day seems so dark
I hear your laugh, and it brightens my night.

When things seem quiet
And I'm left to my thoughts,
I look up, see you and feel peace
Instead of worrying.

Although you've been around
I couldn't admire your light until now.
I'm forever grateful.

As much as you say I brighten your day,
I can always look to you to brighten my night.

My moonlight.

MY MIDNIGHT SKY

I saw her,
and I loved her instantly.
But it wasn't her outer beauty I saw;
it was the confidence and grace
that came with being loved by the moon.
It was captivating.
And to think,
she chose to love me too.

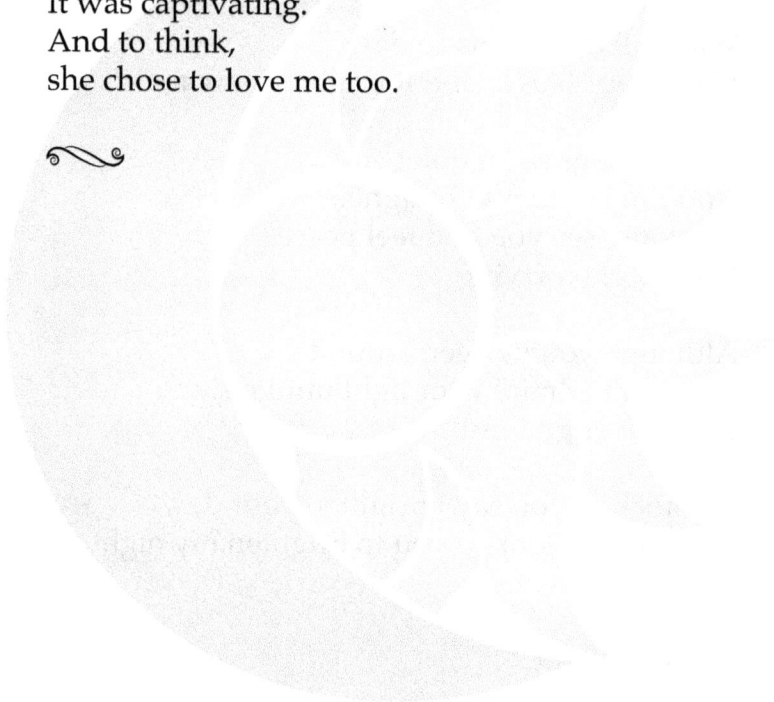

STILL

You can have all the love in the world in your
    heart to give.
Still, you'll want someone to love you back.
You can tell me self-love is enough and
yes, it's most definitely a must.
Still, you'll need someone to love you back.
Eventually…

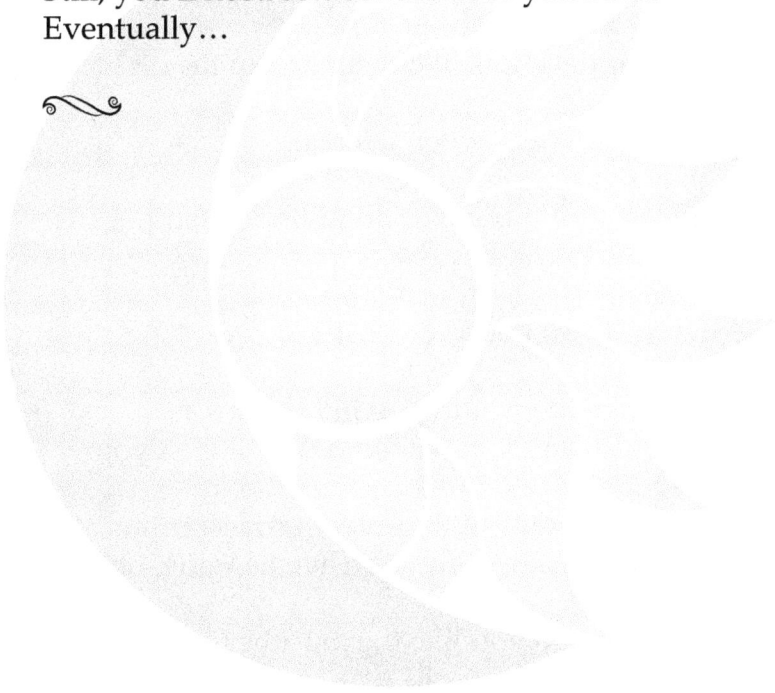

ONE DAY SUNSHINE

One day you'll see your love,
and your eyes will see into his soul.
And his soul will speak to your heart telling it...

"It's time to wake up.
It's time to open up and let me love you.
It's time to let me shine
into your darkness like the moon in the night."

And you'll know when it's real.
It may not always be right
in the eyes of those that don't understand,
but you'll know.

How will you know, you ask?

You'll imagine waking up in his arms
with a kiss on the forehead, and it'll melt your
    soul.
He'll make you feel like every imperfection
is beautiful. Hair a mess, weave hanging, no
    makeup.
Then he'll kiss you like the most beautiful
    person in the world.

And even on days when he doesn't feel at his
    best,
you'll quickly remind him
that you deserve the opportunity to love him

in the good, the bad, and the worse.
With his stinky morning breath.

One day you'll meet your best friend
out of nowhere, and you'll find passion
that you never knew you could have.
One day Sunshine.

But please don't confuse the stars with the
    moonlight.
You'll know when you know,
and he'll make it clear.

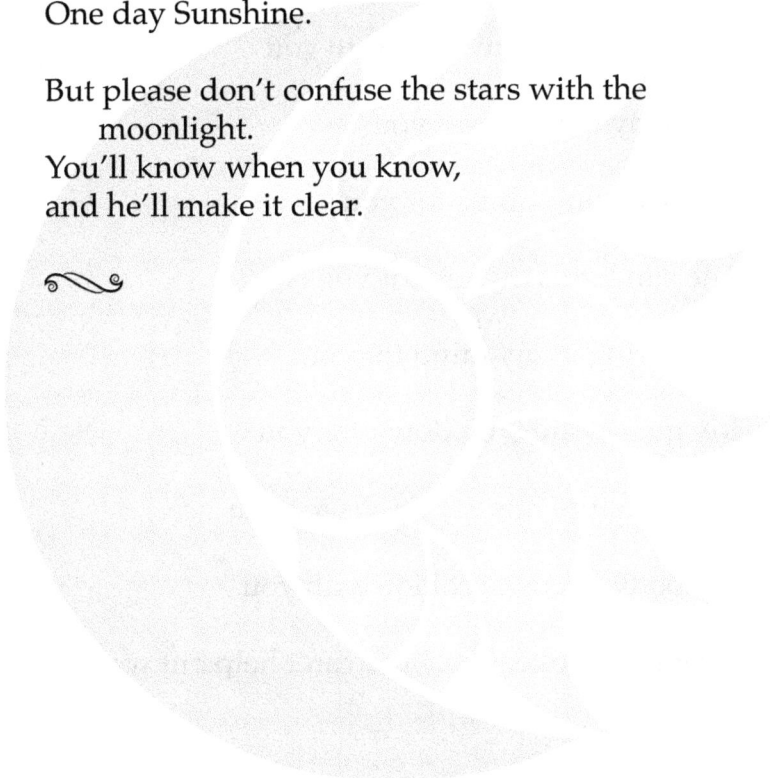

ONLY YOU

My heart only beats for you

My soul only knows you

My mouth tells my secrets to you

My body only misses you

The stars only shine for you

The sun lights my fire for you

Songs ring in my mind for you

My guards are only down for you

The moisture hits my thighs for you

My body opens to collide with you

I think it's unhealthy, but I can't help but want
only you

SOLAR ECLIPSE

It's so easy to fall in love with sunshine.
It warms you and reminds you of a brighter day.
It tells you that no matter how much rain,
it'll always shine again.

It smiles,
even when no one else is smiling back.
It's golden in the most beautiful way.
It brings hope to any situation.

Its light is so bright to the point
where it becomes unbearable.

It never lets anyone close
because it realizes with beauty
usually comes pain.

So, it settles,
never truly close to anything it loves
in fear of destroying it.
But it's always there
to shine on your beautiful face.

This was the most beautiful love story I had ever
    written...

Until I met the moonlight.

The way it gazed into my soul
reminding me it was OK to let go.

Calming me through the night.
Giving vision to the darkness.
Seeing stars with every passionate kiss.
Understanding every story untold
because it saw dreams in the clouds of my mind.
It listens when no one else is around.

It tells my sunshine...

"Rest. I got you through the night.
Let me ease the burden of being everyone's light.
I'll let you so close
you can give the love you never could.
I'll tell the stars of their mother's beauty
until the day we can finally be.
I'll love you from here."

You are my moonlight
and I am your sunshine

SOULMATE

I love you
In your entirety
I've known you
For as long as I can remember
Even though I've just met you
Our souls once danced to a love song
That only they knew the words to
Every time I'm near you
I can feel them pulling near one another
It's undeniable
Yet we fight it
Why?
Why can't we just give in
To what we need
To what needs to be
To what knows its destiny
A destiny where we collide
As one
For indefinitely

BLAZE

If heat wasn't hot
It would still be spicy.
If remember meant forgot,
You would still ignite me.

If the beat never dropped
You would still excite me.
If I seek and you would hide
You'd still find me.

If my sun blazed the night
You'd still be shining.
If hello meant goodbye,
We'd keep goodbye on repeat.

SOULMATES AREN'T FOREVER

Sometimes your soulmate
was never meant for you to have and to hold.
Sometimes your soulmate
was there to allow you to love them enough to
    remind you that you still could.
Sometimes your soulmate was there
to show you how you could and should be loved.

Sometimes your soulmate's only job
was to give you a break from being so strong.
Even if just for a moment,
allow you to believe they've got you;
Like they would protect you and lead you to
    your true self.

What if your soulmate
was just there to help you see the beauty
of the sunlight within yourself?
To unlock the part of you,
you could never trust with anyone else.
The part that was too bright for even you
when you were darkest.

What if you were only there to show them
just how amazing they were?
To appreciate the person they've become.
To allow them to be comfortable and free
even if just for a moment.

What if your only job
was to allow them to find a friend
that would love them forever,
just to give them back?
Because truly, you were both on borrowed time.

Oh, how I wish soulmates were forever.

YOU WOULDN'T TAKE A CHANCE

Perfect is subjective to the person,
and you were my person.

Beauty is to who creates it
and you were created for me.

Destiny can only be made in darkness but
    survived in light,
I was your sunshine, and you were my
    moonlight.

Souls always remember their mate,
and mine still dances with yours.

Life is all about the choices we make,
Truthfully, we never really had a chance.

Nothing happens by chance but by choice,
and you wouldn't take a chance... for me.

THEY ALWAYS COME BACK

At some point, you're going to want me.
All that I tried to give to you.
All that I wanted to be for you.

You'll wake up one day with a void
after you've chased and loved the other's
    attention,
and that won't be enough. Ask me how I know.

You'll miss me.
You'll call me back so suddenly
to see if I miss you too.

And I won't. So, don't.

LEAVE ME OR LOVE ME

Sometimes the best way to love someone
is to let them go.

Sometimes the best way to show them,
is to do what they love you too much to do.

Sometimes you see how much damage you've
    done,
and you just can't stand to see them hurt that
    way.

Sometimes you regret it because maybe
you should have loved them back to health
& help fix the heart you broke.

Just maybe.

BE PATIENT WITH ME

There is no peace in patience.
No matter how you look at it.

There is only anticipation knowing what could
    be
or hoping for what you want.

There is only frustration not knowing why you
    must wait
and not caring at the same time.

Then there is the disappointment
of all the time wasted and all that would have
    been.

Next, excitement from the good of the two evils
which sends you and your heart into a part.

Either way, there is no peace.

It is cruel to tell someone you love to wait or
    hold on
because you know they will.

It is also cruel to tell them to leave
knowing they won't let go.

So how do you fix it?
You grow sooner than later.

You decide that the better version of you
is deserved by the better version of them.

You only find peace when you conquer fear.
Fear of change, fear of growth,
fear of letting go to start something new.

∾

IN SOME WAY, IT'S MY FAULT

Imagine envying your own beauty
because even with how beautiful you are
it was never enough to save your heart from
    hurt.

Imagine blaming yourself
for even putting yourself in that situation, to
    begin with.
Knowing you were never enough to change his
    mind,
let alone his heart.

Imagine crying until no more tears could fall
because you knew better.

And as heartbroken as you are, you can't help
    but think
"she can't possibly love him the way I do.
Does she?"

LEARN YOUR LOVE FOR ME

No need to learn me…
you know me, fully.
A purity no one could defy.

Learn your love for me.
Learn to be OK,
with how you feel about me.

Learn to love the person
you become with me.

Love shouldn't always be expressed outwardly.
True love is loving the form of you
I inspire you to be.

I WAS WRONG

I thought I was OK with the entire situation.
I thought I was strong enough to wait for you to
    choose me.
I thought I could love you while you still loved
    her.
I was wrong.

I thought I didn't need you to come home to me.
I thought I was so much better than the woman
    you lay next to.
I thought I was everything you ever wanted and
    needed.
I shouldn't have.

Because at some point, you loved her.
At some point every day, you chose her over me.
You chose to kiss her and make love to her
and fall asleep in her arms.
While I'm home missing you.

You chose wrong.

THE START TO THE END

Hate to say I felt it happening

Eventually, he forgot to call back more often than
he remembered.

Soon enough, he forgot to tell you goodnight sunshine,

knowing it was the highlight of your night.

At some point, he told you "no" more than he told
you "yes."

Somewhere down the line,

he stopped longing to see your smile & hear your
laugh.

In time you started to mourn him, although he
never said goodbye.

It'll hurt once you notice he lost the sparkle in his eyes.

It'll kill you when you realize you're no longer the
sun in his sky.

It'll blind you when you see he gave up being your
moonlight.

THE POWER OF TOUCH

I love brail.
Not that I understand it,
I just love how touch
can mean so much to a person.

Once your touch lost its feeling,
I felt like you lost your meaning.
Then I knew it wasn't long
before you'd leave me.

It's best I detach now.

SHOOTING STAR

Dear shooting star,
There is no safe   place to land.
Just keep flying.

But can you fly by me one more time?

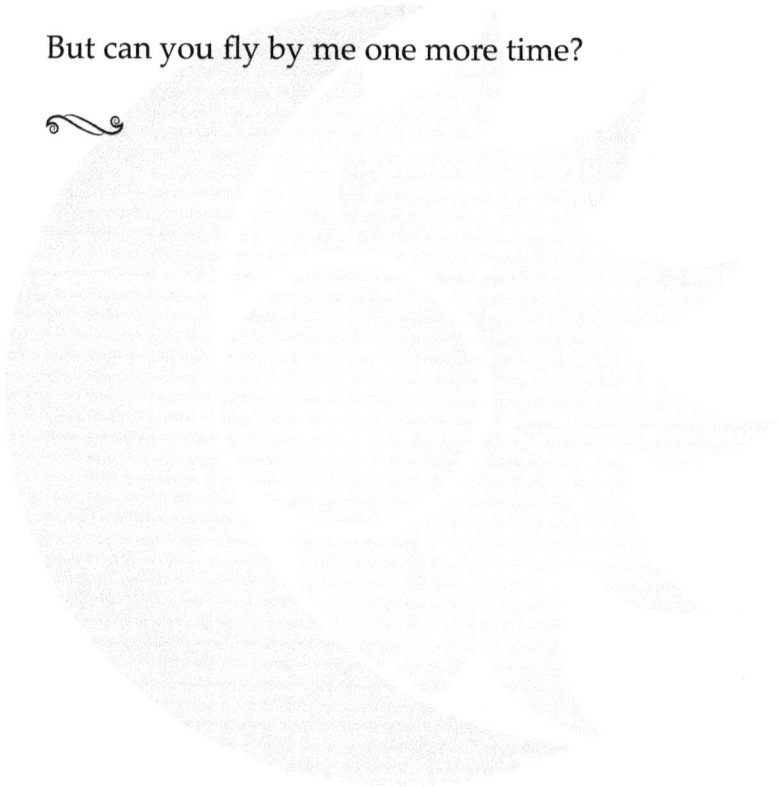

MY WISH

If I had a wish right now;

It wouldn't be that I never met you.
Because I really don't regret you.
That's more than I can truly grasp.

It wouldn't be that inside you're dead too.
Like Romeo and Juliet do.
I'm not dramatic enough for that.

It'd be that you never showed me
How much you really adored me,
If you couldn't maintain that shit!

IT'S OK

Tonight, I picked a pen to write all the emotions
    I was feeling,
and more tears hit the paper than actual words,
    and that's OK.

Sometimes the greatest poems are written in
    tears
and the greatest prayers are said in pain.

FUCK THE GOOD GUY

I asked you to make a choice,
and the moment I did that, the choice was
    already made.
The moment you said you couldn't
was the moment I knew I could never really be
    your choice.
I could only be the thing you longed for at night.
I could only be the beautiful, forbidden fruit.

See, we were never meant to meet, only to exist
as one, connected by the sky
but at two different times.
My time was day, yours night.

Me asking you to choose was me asking you
to leave the stars and eclipse with me.
It was the perfect romance. But it was
    impossible.
Because you never needed the stars, they needed
    you.
That's what you loved about them.
Without you, they were nothing, and that made
    you feel good.

I, on the other hand, could light the sky alone.
Much like you. And I did it well.
That's what attracted you to me, my flame.
You gave me a chance to rest while you lit the
    sky for a while,

that's why I loved you.
You saw my beauty when others just got burned
     and blind trying.
You let me be vulnerable
while everyone else expected me to be so bright.

I could show you my darkest parts
and you loved them the same.
I knew you'd never leave the stars
because you were too afraid
to let someone love and appreciate you the right
     way.
You would rather be what makes everyone else
     happy
instead of allowing yourself to be free with me.
And in some fucked up form of this,
that makes you feel good about yourself.
Being the good guy.

This is why the sun shines alone.
Because while you, the moon, has a choice
to be broken & beautiful, incomplete & lovely.
I have to be whole with no choice.
Until we meet again in the solar eclipse.

I'D WAIT FOREVER, BUT I WON'T

I would love to tell you I'd wait a thousand
    years.
But I can't.
I would love to say I'll be the person you want
    and change.
But I won't.
If you truly love someone, you should never
    want them to change
the person they are.
I believe I am enough just the way I am
for you to love me wholeheartedly.
Because with all that you are and all that you
    aren't,
I loved you and wanted you.
I understand now that I can never truly love you
until I love myself enough to realize
I deserve better than what you want to give me.
I can't love half of you with all of me.

NON-EXISTENT

The more I tried to convince myself
that your love doesn't exist.
The less I needed convincing.

Your love haunted me
like monsters in my dreams.
Once I woke up, I realized
that neither exists.

So I decided to chase something real.
My own love.

HAPPY FOR YOU

You were supposed to miss me forever.
You were supposed to change for me.
You were supposed to be lonely and hurt
for the pain you caused me.

You were supposed to be a better man
with me or not at all.
You weren't supposed to love her better.
You weren't supposed to give her everything I
    deserved.
You weren't supposed to make it easy to love
    you
when I went through hell.

How is it that you're happy before I'm healed?
Life can't possibly be fair.
How can my heart still be dying
while you're living?

I don't want your pity,
I wanted your pain.
But I guess I'll lie and say I'm happy for you.
So that you don't win
And know just how bad you really messed me
    up.

IT WASN'T ALL BAD

I won't say it was all bad.
That'd be a lie.
I won't say you were a monster.
You were once my guy.

I won't say our love only brought pain.
You were my only reason to smile.
I won't say you left me with nothing.
You gave me your first child.

I'll never say you didn't love me,
or else this wouldn't hurt so bad.
I won't say we weren't headed for forever,
which makes me so goddamn mad.

I won't say I don't still love you,
God knows I always will.
I just hate the hole you left in me,
and how long it's taking to heal.

MY MOTHER'S HEART

My mother's heart taught me how to love.
It wasn't always right
or anything I aspired to be,
but it never ran out of love.

No matter how hurt it got.
No matter how bad it broke.
It was never too broken
or ever too empty
to love me.

Unconditionally,
Undeniably,
Incomparably.

MY MOTHER LOVED A MAN

My mother loved a man
that had dreams bigger than his heart,
but he gave her a son that gave her a new start.

My mother had a man
she was too damaged to love back,
but he left her with a daughter.
So beautiful, yet damaged, with hair down her back.

My mother trusted a man
who could only love himself
and whatever woman came along.
He left her with a daughter.
Tough as could be, never trusting anyone.

My mother married a man
he said it would never happen again.
She left him and took the two boys
and a girl that would change the world.

My mother loved her kids
Three boys and three girls. They were her soul.
She taught those kids a lesson,
that love wasn't worth your soul.

Because my mother loved a man
she was never alone.
Sometimes I wish she was
so that she could find love on her own.

HER MENTALITY

I spoke to a friend in a situation similar to my
    own.
I asked why she stayed.
Her response was simple but so complex.
I hated that I even understood it even more
    related to it.

She said that she had told him,

"Do what you're going to do to hurt me.
Just don't be a cost and leave me hurting."

❧

ISSUES

It's funny how those abandonment issues
transfer into relationship issues.
Sometimes, I wonder if I don't want to lose you
    because I want you
or if I'm just afraid you'll leave like everyone
    else.

I guess this healing thing goes deeper than I
    thought.

VALUABLE

Expect nothing for the love you give.
Give it because it's in you to do so.

Don't accept nothing.
There is a difference.

Your love is valuable and powerful
and should be treated as such.

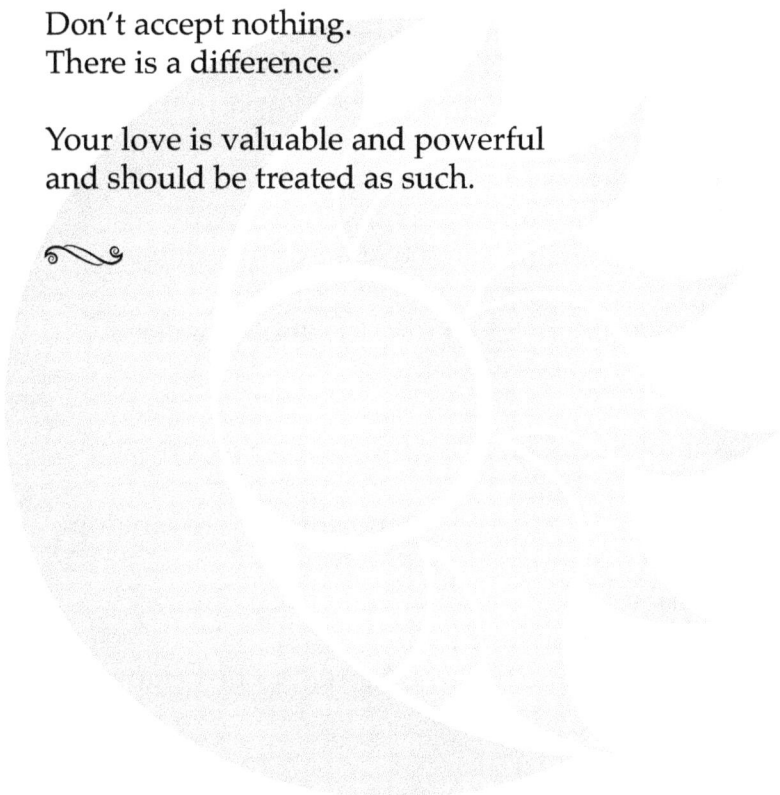

I WAS NEVER ENOUGH

I was willing to look crazy going through your
    phone.
I was willing to make right everything I did
    wrong.
I was trying to heal the pieces of your love.
I was trying to force even the simplest of hugs.

I really did want the fairytale life.
I really did deserve the title of your wife.
I honestly would have waited until you were
    done hurting me.
That would've taken forever; you're never
    satisfied with anything.

You told me so much how everything about me
    was wrong.
That I had learned the tune and started singing
    the same song.
I started to ask myself, "Why can't you just
    make him happy?"
Until that quickly turned into "If I just change
    one more thing…"

It took years before I realized I would never be
    enough.
It took forever before I did it and finally called
    your bluff.
That lasted for a while, but then there was
    everything that I deserved;

Being handed to someone new as if she had been
    there through the worst.

You built her up and showed her off as if she
    made you feel proud.
Still, you found a way to break my heart while
    carrying your last child.
Then I tried again. I fought my deepest fears; I
    just wanted my family whole.
But your hurt surpassed mine, as if your bullets
    fell shy and didn't pierce my soul.

You turned to me with a puffed-up chest "you
    should have just accepted my mess."
So instead, you gave someone you barely know
    your best,
and you left me with only memories of the rest.

LOVE WHAT WE LACK

Often we love what we lack.
Like how you were everything I wasn't.
Which made me love you more
To somehow fill the pieces I was missing.
It's really brilliant if you think about it,
A recipe for a perfect fit.
But what happened is the parts of you
Started to change parts of me,
And parts of me started to destroy parts of you.

EPIPHANY

Before you know it
you'll look up
years later
wondering what you've allowed
to happen to you.

BREATHE

Breathe,

Cry,

Release.

As many times as it hurts.

As much as you can.

And then do something about it.

It doesn't matter how long it takes.

CYCLE OF HEALING

Live
{you wake up every day to try again}

Feel
{allow your soul to feel whatever it feels, even if
    it makes no sense}

Trust
{we all break promises, the worst ones to
    ourselves, trust that you'll do better}

Question
{never doubt yourself but always question what
    doesn't feel right}

Let go
{sometimes we forgive, sometimes we don't, but
    for the love of peace, please let it go}

Die
{when you lay your head down, the old you
    dies daily; who you choose to be when you
    awake is up to you}

Repeat.....
{no matter what happens or how it hurts, life is
    about learning and doing it again but better}

YOU'RE NEVER TOO DAMAGED

One day God will see your heart
with every dent, bruise, strain, and mistake.
He'll love it enough
to connect it with its mate.

That only happens when you release
all the leeches and soul ties to people and things
that mean you no good
and do you no good
even if it feels good.

You were never too damaged to be loved
just too premature in healing to receive it.

SOUL TIES

Just another number in your phone, maybe even
    one of the favorites.
Another woman to please your moans, maybe
    even one of the best.
None of that means anything.

The moment I said no, another says yes.
The moment I let go, another is calling next.

Perhaps that's why some stay in fear of losing
    their place.
Perhaps they'd rather feel momentary relevance
    or live up to some name.
Perhaps they don't recognize their beauty or the
    value of the soul.

Because wherever that man lays, his soul picks
    up ghosts.
And you wonder why you ponder when you
    should be asleep.
You wonder why you think of them, and it
    disturbs your peace.

They say that dogs give you fleas, and you get
    bugs when you shake trees.

WHITE ROSES

You don't smell the same anymore.
I used to hug you & feel your heartbeat,
it doesn't beat the same anymore.
I used to trust that we were family, no matter
    what;
you don't care for me anymore.
I used to know that I could always cry in your
    arms,
I don't feel safe with you anymore.
I used to think you'd go to war behind me.
I can't see past all the tears.
I used to see the good in all the bad.
You don't smell the same anymore,
what used to be red roses now smell like white
    ones.

HELLO STRANGER

I remember when I knew you.
I remember when I felt you.
I remember when I adored you.
Hello stranger.

WHAT KIND OF SHIT IS THAT?

You broke my heart then asked me why I was so
 hurt.

You betrayed my soul then told me to trust your
 plan.

You left me confused but hate when I ask
 questions.

COMPLICATED

It's not complicated.
We overthink things
so we can come up with some kind of logic
that makes sense.
Some reason to explain the level of messed up
    you feel.
I mean, there must have been some long back
    story
as to why I got played.
Right?
But some part of healing is accepting that there
    isn't.
Accepting that you just weren't that important.
To them anyway.
You just didn't even matter in the moments of
    betrayal.
Sometimes things really do just happen.
Sometimes your heartbreak isn't a big deal.
There is no reason why
or explanation to ease the hurt
or make any sense.
We want things to be complicated
to save our minds from tormenting us.
At some point, you have to come to terms with
    the fact that
it's just not.

I'll be ok
Just give me time to forget.

FORGET TO LOVE YOU

I never needed a reason to hate you
or push you away.
Once I stopped finding reasons to love me
I knew you couldn't possibly.

I guess the mind games and manipulation
    backfired.
Now that I'm too busy looking for reasons to
    love me,
I forget why I love you.

THEIR TRUTH, YOURS AND MINE

I remember my mother telling a story
from everyone's perspective involved.
Then she told the same story
from the bystander who knew nothing at all.

Your truth was that I broke your heart.
My truth is that I healed mine.
Your truth was that I broke a bond.
My truth is that family never dies.

Your truth was there was so much to hide.
My truth is that I needed time.
Your truth was that all I told was lies.
My truth is that you only saw it from your eyes.

Your truth was that I never made an effort.
But I gave everything left in my heart.
The only truth that matters now
is that we have come to the point to depart.

DRIFT

We were at sea
but the tides got heavy
it didn't scare me...
at first.

I can stand the waters
and the lightning bolts.
I can stand the uneasy rocks
of the boat we shared.

I can stand the dark clouds
that came rolling in,
but as soon as the sea gets calm
here the storm comes again.

But the boat
Was fragile at best.
It was old and unsteady;
Put together with sticks and stones.

We used whatever we could find
to clog the leaks.
Covering every fear
with temporary fixes.

Until the winds got heavy
we floated along just fine,
but the waters got troubled
and I saw it in our eyes.

The boat tore apart
no matter how much we tried
to hold it all together,
a fate we knew would come.

So, I drifted.

You called out for me,
but the silence was too loud.
I could see you,
but the clouds were in my eyes.

I couldn't feel you, though,
not the good in you anyway.
Only the fear, the hurt, and the pain.
They came rushing like waves.

But you wouldn't let me help you
so, I kept drifting
and you kept calling
until you realized I was gone.

I was safe ashore
with nothing left but my heart.
I was safe but lonely
but healing.

But you were stuck.

It hurt to know
I couldn't save you.
It helped to know
I was never supposed to.

CHAOS IN MY HEAD

I can't save you.
I can't handle that responsibility.
My chest burns, and my head aches
With the simplest thought of it.
If you're looking to me for your peace,
I can't!

It's too chaotic in my own head,
but I've just made music of it.
If you're looking to me for strength,
I'm weak!

Trust me; my bite
isn't near as big as my bark.
I just stay ready for anything,
like a runner on her mark.

If you need to trust me,
you shouldn't!

I'm unpredictable and unstable.
My intentions never match my actions,
but I must protect my soul.
So I'll always throw the first blow.

It's fair if I let you know.
If you want to love me still,
Why?!

I'm damaged and probably can't love you the
    same.
If I could, I probably wouldn't,
Just to stay sane.
There is just as much chaos in my heart,
as there is in my mind.

MY CHOICE, PLEASE

Truth is, I needed you
just as much as you needed me.
Difference is I didn't want to.
I wanted to be free from you,
So I could willingly love you.
Not because I was afraid of you.
Not because you made me feel like
I shouldn't be happy without you.
I wanted to leave you
so I could be free to love you.
The way I wanted to.
Not the way that involved me
being property of you.
I wanted to be free to choose you.
I don't like when you make decisions for me.

I never needed you to save me.
I just wanted you there
while I saved myself

THE LESSON OF THE SEA

You may never change
the directions of the waves
or calm the roaring sea.

You may never understand
why the storm came
or just how long it'll be.

But just as long
as you accept the change
you'll learn the lesson of the sea.

To hold freedom and peace
you must endure the storm,
that's serenity.

I WAS FREE

I stopped blaming myself
for the bitterness inside you.
Now I can finally focus
on the happiness inside me.

Then I was free.

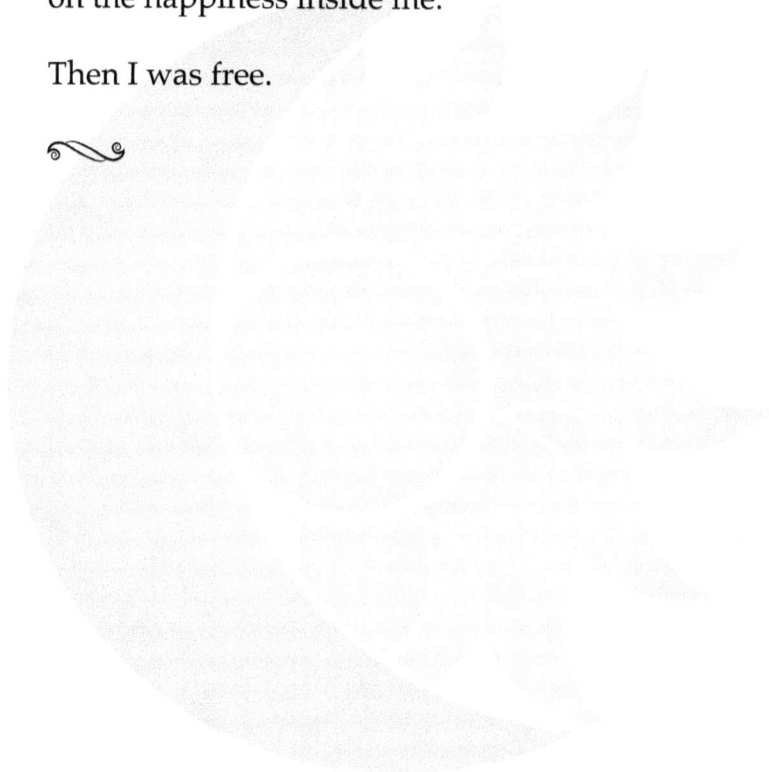

I ALMOST

I almost fell back into that old thing
On a fling
I almost fell into those brown eyes
Forgot the lies
I almost laid down next to you
Something sexual
I almost did the things I said I never would
Nothing good
I almost forgot the pain I felt at night
Was not alright
I almost forgot the reason I left you behind
No longer blind
Then I quickly remembered you couldn't even
    half love me right
Never mind

JUST WHEN I PULLED AWAY

I tried! I really did.
But I couldn't stop seeing your face.
My heart wouldn't stop beating at your pace.
My soul wouldn't stop calling your name.

I cried. I swear I did.
But the tears were as sweet as your kiss.
Your warmth and touch I miss.
I can't believe it happened like this.

I died. It felt like it.
When I couldn't hold you at night.
When all I asked was for you to choose right.
I kept thinking you didn't even try.

I pulled away. For good, I guess.
But you came back and showed me love.
You came back, and I got stuck.
You came back to love for us.

Just when I pulled away,
you came back and tried to make me stay.
But you couldn't because I was done.

COVER UP

I'm starting to see my freedom
Irritate your captivity.

THE SAND BENEATH MY FEET

"Sit here; we're safe here,"
said the sand beneath my feet.
"Sink here, embrace here.
Deep breath, close your eyes. Don't speak.
Imagine it, a life of no troubles,
only the sounds of birds and waves.
You can have it, the life you wanted
of peace and serenity all day."

I'm sorry, love, sounds amazing,
but the wind is calling my name.
It's my destiny, my fate, you see.
The wind gives life to my flame.

"But you can dance with me.
I'll wash your feet
with the beautiful water
of the sea".

Our time must end
Until forever my friend
My feet don't belong in the sand.
I was always meant to be free
And to dance with the wind.

YOU DON'T SEE IT NOW

One day your heart won't hurt for me.

One day it'll only feel love.
One day you'll know that I never meant you any
     harm
and that understanding me was a challenge in
     itself.

One day you'll see me smile
and you'll know it's because I'm proud
of your growth and the strength you've always
     had.

One day you'll forgive the pain
and you'll see the purpose,
or you won't, but you'll be content anyway.

One day.

One day you'll love you enough
to know that I could never be your happiness
even if I laid down my life.

One day I hope you wrap your arms around me
 and feel my genuine love for you
instead of every stupid thing I did to hurt you.

One day I hope you're healed enough
to forgive me for trying to love you
before I healed myself.

MY GIFT

I hurt you, I know.
Not more than I hurt myself.
I kept you unsure,
Of the truth behind how I felt.

My gift should be my love.
That's all you said you wanted.
My gift should be my honesty.
My lies still keep you haunted.

I'll give you the one gift,
I know you'll never keep.
I'll gift you with my absence.
The key to the peace you need.

SOMEONE IS ME

We tell ourselves
"If someone would just love me,
then I would be better".

But it doesn't work that way.

You take all power from yourself,
and further you're asking
to damage someone else.

Everyone deserves a moment
to be selfish.
But not like that.
Not at the cost of someone else.

That's what's wrong with humanity now.
We ask for what we're incapable of giving.
Draining the love from someone else.

Leaving a bunch ofincapable, unhealed, loveless
    people
Looking for someone to love them.

Simply put

don't fuck me up trying to fix you.

HOW'D YOU KNOW?

I wasn't good or happy alone.
That's how I knew I wasn't ready to be happy
    with you.
You have to know that me hurting you
had nothing to do with you.

HATE ME

If it takes you hating me to get back,
then do it. I'll bear the burden of that.
If it takes you to scream, cry and yell,
then go for it, I'll stand back.
If you want to give up and sit in misery,
I'll give you about 10 seconds flat.
Just understand that you can't stay there,
I won't sit around for that.

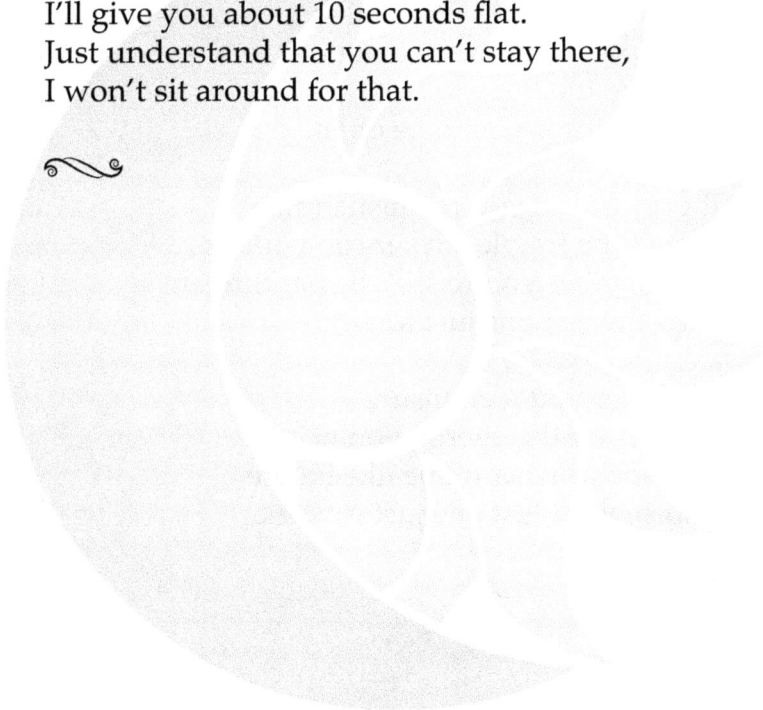

THE LAST ONE

You told me about your past.
The things you still cope with.
I figured out your math.
The equation to all you hold in.

I'll hold you while you heal.
I'll support your every emotion.
When it's too deep to feel.
I'll never force you to be open.

I'll pray for all you're mishandling.
I'll read the fragile stickers on your box.
I'll remember you're still dismantling.
While the last one just forgot.

Whenever you feel unsure
I'll give you the energy you need.
Just know this won't be like before
Because your last one just isn't me.

HEALING IS MY RESPONSIBILITY

Healing doesn't mean
not hurting anymore.
That's silly.
What makes you healed,
is when you can still love,
With the same intensity,
the same power,
through your hurt,
knowing you could get hurt again.
Knowing this person
is not responsible for my past,
and only I am responsible for my future.

BEAUTIFUL SOUL

When you meet someone with a beautiful soul,
Appreciate it!
Tell them!
Show them!
Because this world will give you
so many reasons to be ugly.

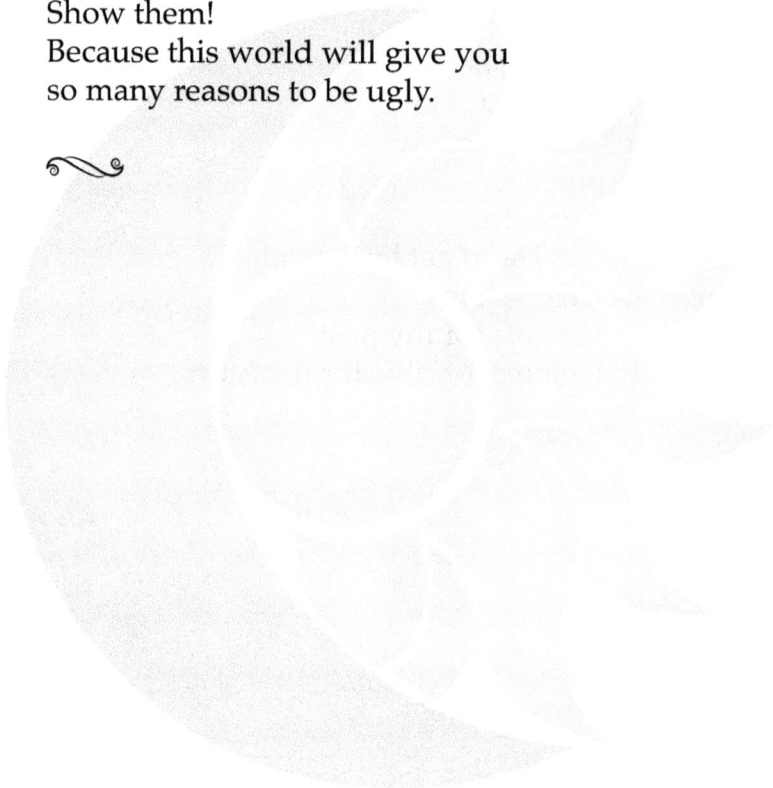

PERPLEX

This memory of mine
Is selective at best
I heard the suggestions
From those who know best

They said you'd moved on
I should let you go now
It was cliché, but truth is
I didn't know how

They, those and them
Had no idea where to go
Them, they and those
Only filled my head with no

No, don't distract him
He's become a new man
No, don't attract him
Like only you can

The man may be new
His soul preserved as mine
The man may have her
His heart was my design

He knew me, mine, ours
Hidden for sake and sanity
The curve, the cave, the being
Knew with you was clarity

He had what was impossible
Peace in my absence
He had what he needed
The absence of passions

Me free from him
He was safe from me, finally
They eventually noticed
Neither wanted to be, really

I learned to forget
He learned to suppress
I guess them, they and those
Always knew best

They
never

knew
best.

LET'S MEET HERE AGAIN

When the time comes for us to revisit this love,
remember a few things for me:

Remember how broken we were inside and
    never told the other.
Remember the love we let die when I was lost in
    being a mother.
Remember how our hearts held every mistake
    and grasped every wrong.
Remember how much better we are now and
    never let it get that far gone.

Let's love each other fully and whole while we
    never stop loving ourselves.
Let's meet here again when you can look at me
    and smile.

Even if it's simply as friends.
And maybe, just maybe, this love thing will be
    worthwhile.

A FOOL

I'd be a fool to meet there again.
Knowing the outcome,
Knowing how bad it could hurt.
Again!

CHANGE YOUR HEART

People don't change.
Their hearts may,
But they don't.

They are still capable of those terrible things.
They just don't have the heart or will to do them
  anymore.

So when I tell you that I've changed,
See my heart's posture.

REPEAT LESSON

Life will teach you every lesson
If you live long enough.
It may even teach you twice
Just to make your skin tough.

It'll send little reminders
From the first set of mistakes.
If it would have never hurt,
How would you know to appreciate?

It may even teach you over and over
Until you scream, "Enough!"
Now that I've learned my lesson,
Can I just enjoy my love?

ONE MORE TIME

You were the best version of hello
and the worst version ofgoodbye.
Hello, my name is love,
Can we try this one more time?

WE HAVE PEACE NOW

We have peace now.
Although the flames are just as high.
We accept peace now.
Despite the difference in our horizon.
We live in peace now.
Because peace was just a state of mind.

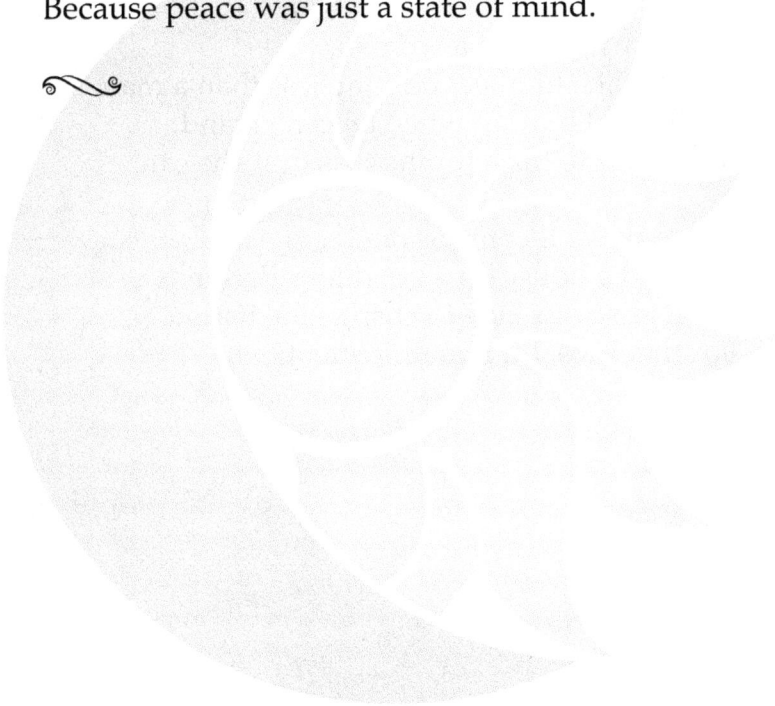

I'LL LOVE A MAN

One day I'll love a man.
He'll rub my back when I'm tired from working.
He'll wipe my tears when I'm tired from
      hurting.
He'll give me peace when I'm uncertain.

One day he'll love a woman.
She'll make him feel nothing less than a man.
She'll hold him up when he can't stand.
She'll add to his happiness as best she can.

One day we'll come as one,
To build a house on a good foundation.
We'll raise our kids to change the nation.
For that love, I'll remain patient.

DEAR AMBER,

I miss you.
I didn't think it would feel this dark without
  you.
They never tell you that you lose yourself trying
  to find peace.
They don't tell you that you have to find a new
  love for the person you're becoming.
They surely don't tell how very few people
  would be there when the process was over
  if anyone was there at all. They don't put
  it in the fine print that your smile will be
  different, almost unrecognizable. They never
  give a fair warning that the number of tears
  you'd cry could put out a forest fire.

They only tell you to leap, to jump, to have faith.
  All very true but very unrealistic. Your leap
  won't be graceful at all,more like a gallop
  with tons of weights on your shoulders. Your
  jump would be more of a fall - one where
  you fell flat on your face. Your faith would
  be in God pulling you out not having to go
  through it.

I would love to tell you that all this is worth
  it. But some days, it doesn't feel like it is. I
  would like to say this will be the best time of
  your life. But it's your worst days that build
  your character. I would love to say you'd

build enough strength to never hurt again. But one of the best perks is becoming OK with your own vulnerability.

I'm learning to love you, Amber. Day by day, I understand your mistakes. Night by night, I appreciate your tears. Time after time, I see your heart. But eventually, Amber, you'll start to see those hues of yellow jewel turn to gold, and it'll all make sense.

Sincerely, You

TIME

Time is nothing.

Live each end as if it's your last.

Live each beginning as if it's your first.

Everything in between is your time.

Measure life by that.

The sun will continue to set.

The leaves will continue to fall.

Enjoy it all.

But hold on to none of it.

You may miss your next holding onto a moment.

Even then, time doesn't matter,

Because what's meant will happen,

In its perfect moment of imperfection.

DIE TO LIVE

I learned peace only after I learnedheartbreak.
Not when someone else broke my heart
But when I broke my own.

No matter how much I loved another
I could never beat the love I had for myself.
I had forgotten that for a moment.

Anything that I had done to me was because I
   allowed it.
Now, that doesn't excuse the assholes who hurt
   me
it only allows room for growth by accepting my
   own fault.

The power was in me, and once I remembered
   that,
I apologized to myself.
Not with words, but with changed behavior.

I started walking with a little extra pep.
I started feeling beautiful inside and out.
I started taking care of me.
Spending a little extra time with me.

When I died, I lived again as a BOSS!
As a queen. As me.
The better version of me.

Who lives and dies daily
Awaking to the more confident,
happy, peaceful, spontaneous, loving person I
    want to be.

The person who has no boundaries
of the great things that I can accomplish.
Every truth that hurt me healed me.

NOT YET

Today you told me

"Love yourself enough to be loved correctly,
And trust me enough to let me be the one to do
    it."

And I couldn't.
Not yet.

IF YOU KNEW

If you knew how ugly my heart was under this,
would you still love me?

If you knew how weak I was under this strength,
would you still be inspired by me?

If you knew how many tears I've cried under
     this smile,
would you still find me beautiful?

HELLO BEAUTIFUL

Hello Beautiful.
Honestly, that doesn't mean much.
You smile, but the pain is easily covered up. Like
    you're stuck.
No one to trust, but you must. Try beautiful!
    Don't get lost
In the darkness that they say your light breaks
    through.

It's crazy, because who sees the light when the
    light is you?
Who loves the lost that speaks no truth,
Who lies about their true intentions with you?
It's you; you do, beautiful.

But I have body bags too.
Here lies the heart and the soul you once knew.
The good died with all the bad they said about
    you.
The darkness has adopted you.

You're praying, saying, "God come on, come
    through.
I really need you.
My light doesn't seem as bright when I don't see
    you."

And He says,
"It's the strong I give my missions to.

This path I have designed just for you.
And with every single tear, you remain
    beautiful.
Even when you don't feel it, my eye beholds
    you.
You're beauty, I'm the beholder, and there's no
    beast in you.
Your heart and your sou,l I can resurrect those
    too.
Just stop giving it to people who don't deserve
    you.
No man can want a queen unless he is a king
    too."

Hello beautiful. Nice to meet you.

IT TOOK FOREVER

I've finally figured out what I've misunderstood
    this entire time.
That the condition of my heart does not define
    who I am.
If anything, it shows how much I've loved, even
    on my worst days.
It shows how much I can bear before I break.
It shows how much I've learned even through
    my pain.
It shows that I've earned my peace and all my
    insanity.
It shows that I'm the dopest person I will ever
    meet.

THE JOURNEY

The hardest part of the journey to happiness
is coming to terms with unsettling.

Then realizing you have to break the heart
of the person who loves you.

This scares me
because I've never not loved you before.

This hurts me
because I know that I'll have to learn how.

This gives me peace
because I finally have the strength to set you free
from the old toxic version of me.

This kills me
because it's you, and this is the end of us.
But it's necessary on this journey.

UNDERSTANDING OTHERS' HURT

I didn't understand why you couldn't look at
me or talk to me too long after what you
had done. In my mind, the least you could
do was listen to the mess of emotions I
was spilling on you. But God helped me
understand that it is possible for someone to
be hurt, seeing the pain they caused you and
not being able to take it away. And the more
you speak about it, the more it's a reminder
of the part of themselves they're ashamed
of. I couldn't see that you hurt yourself in
hurting me. Even if unintentionally.

Was that my burden to bear? No, but it did help
me to understand.

PURPOSE AFTER PAIN

Don't let your emotions blind your purpose.
Feel what you feel
Cry your tears
But you must heal!

Please.

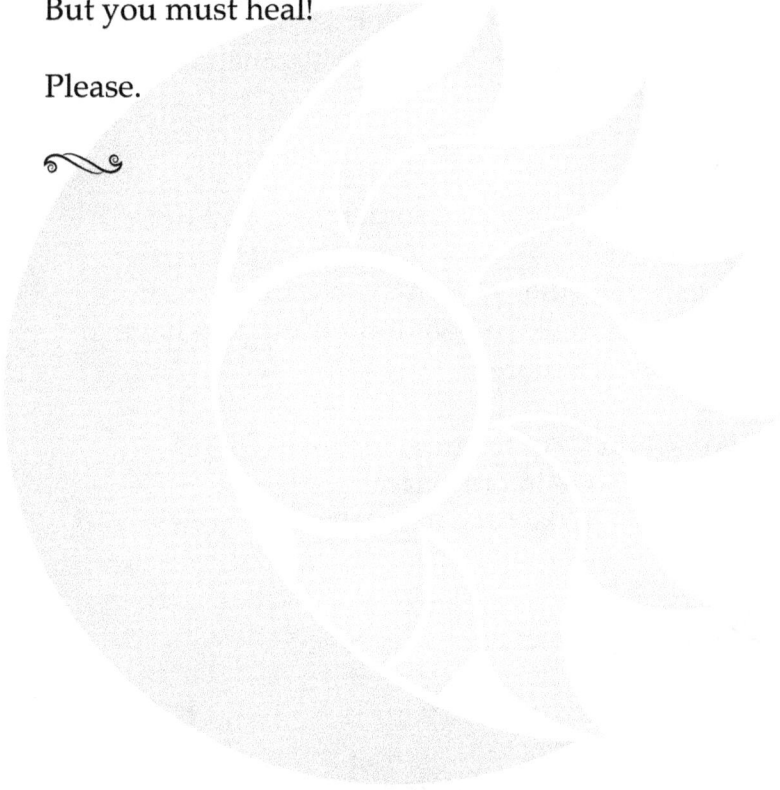

WE ALL DESERVE FORGIVENESS

Sometimes, there is just no way to make things
    right.
Find a way to be OK with that.
Find a way to forgive yourself somehow.

You deserve forgiveness.

Although we're cruel sometimes, and the world
    is cruel,
It's still worth it. Worth the try, the passion.
Worth all the love you don't think you have to
    give anymore.

We spend so much time trying to forget
    everyone in our past,
We don't make time to forgive everyone in our
    past.

"But they never asked for forgiveness!"

Do it anyway. Allow your heart to lift that
    weight.
Or eventually, you'll find yourself mixing that
    hurt
With the hurt from the present.
And healing becomes that much harder.

THANK YOU

Thank you for hurting me.
You ignited something that I would've never
    asked for.
Something that was already inside of me.
Some mantle that I thought was too much for
    me.
At peace with the dark thoughts that I was
    ashamed to see.
A spark to a light that guides my destiny.
It wasn't until I was this hurt that I had the
    strength to be weak.
It wasn't until my worst that I appreciated the
    best about me.
It wasn't until this hurt that I was comfortable
    with being free.
So thank you, and I mean that shit sincerely.

LOVE FREELY

There is no such thing as protecting your heart.

It will love who it wants to love
Even if you know, it's the worst thing for you.

So, love freely and heal frequently.
Appreciate every experience.
Regret nothing.

HOW I KNEW

I was finally happy and good alone.
That's how I knew I was ready to be happy with
    you.
You have to know that my healing
Had nothing to do with you.

JUST PLANT THE SEED

There are no refunds on your soul.
Once it's broken, it's up to you to piece it back
together.
To take whatever is left and build again.

The pieces you left in your past, you will never
get back.
And that's OK because each piece planted a
seed.
Whether it was on good or bad soil is up to
them.

Your job was to plant the seed.
Spark the light.
Maybe it's someone else's job to water and
nurture the seed
Or blow the flame.

Sometimes you'll never get to benefit from the
manifestation
Of your work or see just how big those flames
may get.

But still, life is about planting the seed anyway.
Giving the love anyway.
Lighting the fire in their hearts anyway.
Even if it burns for someone else.

ABOUT THE AUTHOR

Amber L. Graham was born in Detroit, MI and later moved to Houston, TX to finish out her schooling. She's the youngest of 6. Which gained her the nickname "Baby". Growing up, she used writing as a therapeutic way to deal with the loss of her mother and later her brother. This became her escape and expression even in relationships. She'd often enter into contest to showcase her passion. When she isn't writing she's either exploring nature with her children or exploring fashion in her styling business Creatively Tailored. Although she's been writing since young and for other authors, Hello Moonlight... Love, Sunshine is Amber's first book. Like much of her early work, the book captures the journey to healing with the option of love.